DC SUPER HEROES

THE SCIENCE BEHIND
SUPERMAN'S
STRENGTH

by
Agnieszka Biskup

Superman created by
Jerry Siegel and Joe Shuster
by special arrangement with
the Jerry Siegel family

SCIENCE BEHIND
SUPERMAN

CAPSTONE PRESS
a capstone imprint

Published by Capstone Press in 2017
A Capstone Imprint
1710 Roe Crest Drive
North Mankato, Minnesota 56003
www.mycapstone.com

STAR38174

Library of Congress Cataloging-in-Publication Data
Names: Biskup, Agnieszka, author.
Title: The science behind Superman's strength / by Agnieszka Biskup.
Description: North Mankato, Minnesota : Capstone Press, 2016. | Series: DC
    super heroes. Science behind Superman | Audience: Ages 7-9. | Audience: K
    to grade 3. | Includes bibliographical references and index.
Identifiers: LCCN 2016033215 (print) | LCCN 2016039603 (ebook) | ISBN 9781515750994 (library binding) |
    ISBN 9781515751038 (paperback) | ISBN 9781515751151 (eBook PDF)
Subjects: LCSH: Muscle strength—Juvenile literature. | Muscles—Juvenile literature. | Superman
    (Fictitious character)—Juvenile literature.
Classification: LCC QP321 .B5635 2016 (print) | LCC QP321 (ebook) | DDC 612.7/41—dc23
LC record available at https://lccn.loc.gov/2016033215

Summary
Explores the science behind Superman's strength and describes examples of strength from the real world.

Editorial Credits
Aaron Sautter, editor; Veronica Scott, designer; Kelly Garvin, media researcher;
Katy LaVigne, production specialist

Photo Credits
Capstone Press: Erik Doescher, cover, backcover, 1, 3, Luciano Vecchio, 5, 11, 12, 14, 18, Mike Cavallaro, 6,
Min Sung Ku, 22; Getty Images: Bloomberg, 19, Mario Tama, 20; Shutterstock: CLIPAREA/Custom media,
8, David Pegzlz, 16, FXQuadro, 13, martan, 7, Mike Price, 15, Richard Whitcombe, 17, stihii, 10, Valentyna
Chukhlyebova, 9; Warner Brothers, 21

Printed and bound in the USA.
010023S17

Table of Contents

INTRODUCTION
Super-Strength 4

CHAPTER 1
Strong Muscles 6

CHAPTER 2
Animal Strength 14

CHAPTER 3
Strength Enhancements 18

GLOSSARY 22

READ MORE 23

INTERNET SITES 23

INDEX 23

SUPER-STRENGTH

Nobody can match Superman's strength. He can bend solid steel beams. He can even crush diamonds in his hands. But strength isn't limited to super heroes. It's found everywhere from powerful animals to strength-boosting **technology**. The science of strength is all around us.

FACT

Humans have more than 600 muscles in their bodies. These muscles allow people to move in thousands of ways.

technology—the use of science to do practical things

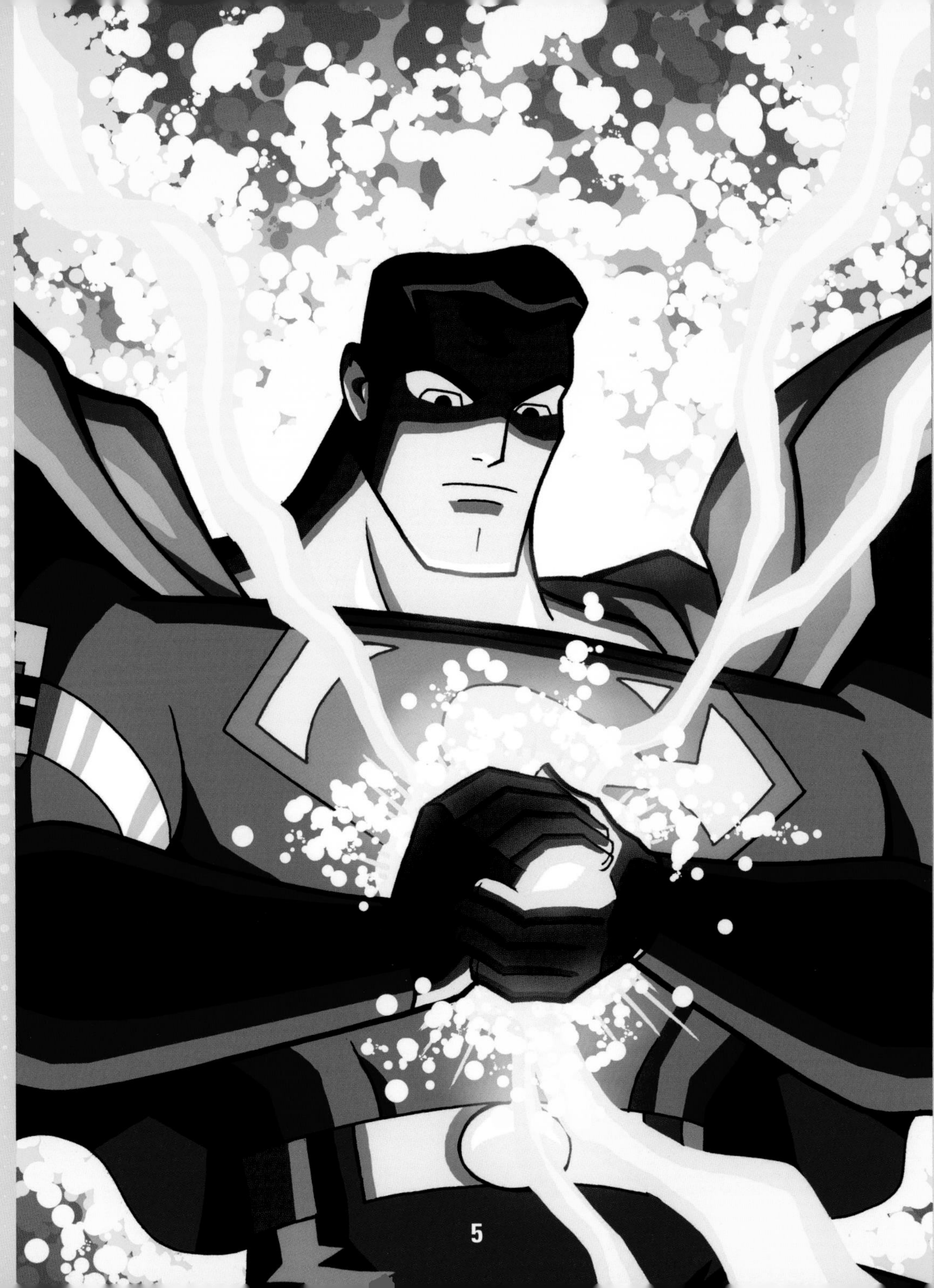

CHAPTER 1

STRONG MUSCLES

Superman's powerful muscles help him do incredible things. Just like him, we use our muscles to create movement.

Smooth, or **involuntary**, muscles move things such as blood or air inside our bodies. Skeletal muscles are **voluntary**. You control them to move your body.

FACT

Eye muscles are the busiest in the body. They may move more than 100,000 times a day!

involuntary—done without a person's control

voluntary—to choose to do something on purpose

Skeletal muscles are connected to your bones by **tendons**. Most bones have more than one muscle attached to them. Muscles usually only work in one direction. Your body needs two or more muscles to move in different directions.

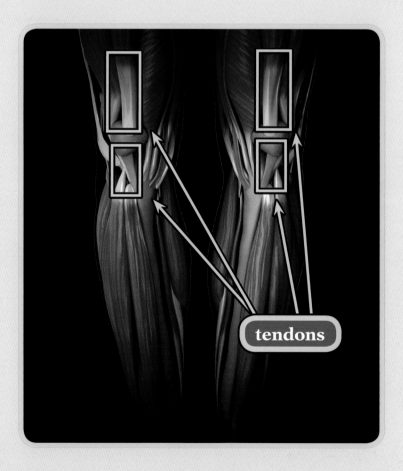

tendons

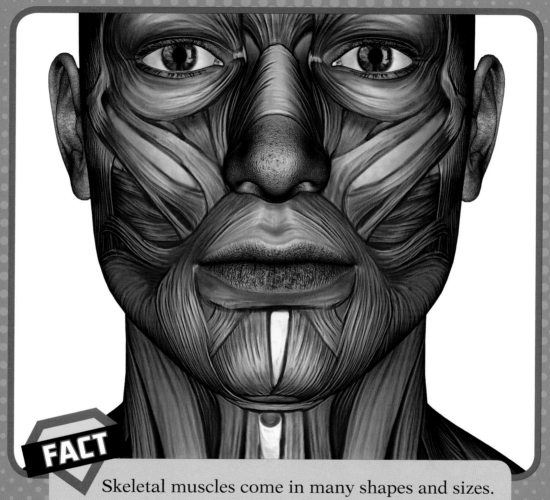

Skeletal muscles come in many shapes and sizes. For example, the muscles around your mouth are circular. They allow you to whistle, talk, and eat.

tendon—a strong, thick cord of tissue that joins a muscle to a bone

Muscles contract and stretch to move your body. When a muscle contracts it gets shorter. It pulls on the bone attached to it. To lift an object, your biceps contracts to pull your arm up. To put it down, you use your triceps muscle. It contracts to lower your arm again.

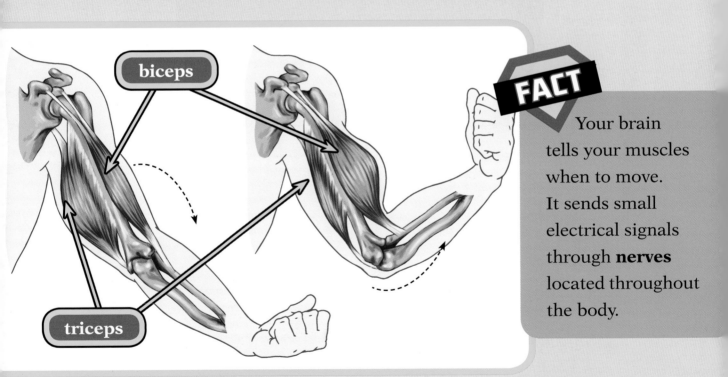

FACT

Your brain tells your muscles when to move. It sends small electrical signals through **nerves** located throughout the body.

nerve—a thin fiber that carries messages between the brain and other parts of the body

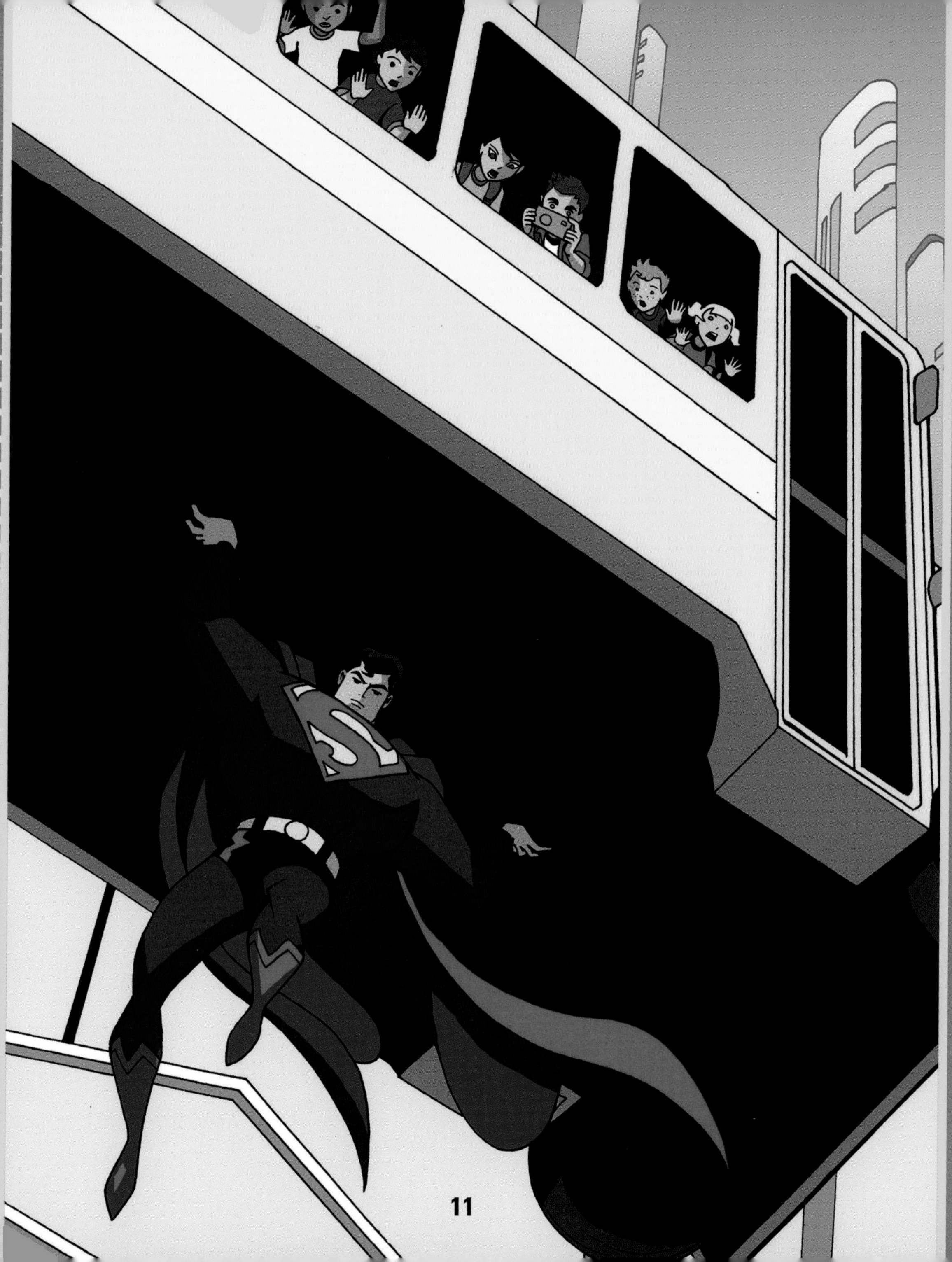

Superman gets his strength from the Sun. But people need to exercise to get stronger. Strength training uses **resistance** to make muscles stronger. Lifting weights forces your muscles to work against **gravity**. The harder they work, the stronger they become.

FACT

Lifting weights causes tiny tears in the muscles. As your body repairs this damage, your muscles grow larger.

resistance—a force that opposes or slows the motion of an object
gravity—a force that pulls objects together

CHAPTER 2

ANIMAL STRENGTH

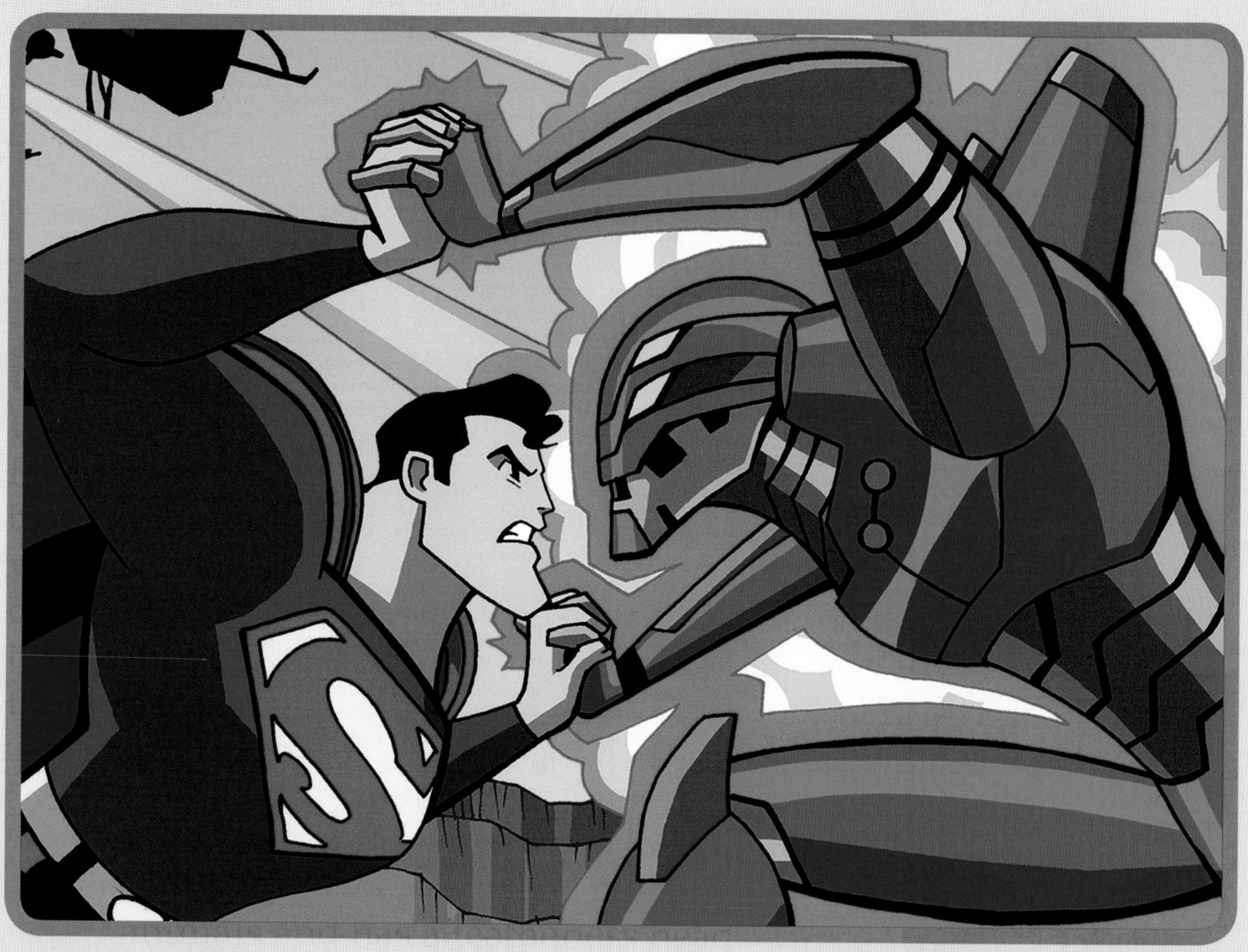

Superman's strength is often the difference between life and death. Strength is important for many animals too. Gorillas are the world's largest apes. Adult male gorillas are six times stronger than an average man. A gorilla can lift as much as 4,400 pounds (2,000 kilograms).

FACT

African elephants are the world's largest land animals. An adult elephant can carry close to 20,000 pounds (9,070 kg)!

Superman packs a mighty punch. But some tiny animals are also incredibly strong. The horned dung beetle is the strongest insect on Earth. It can pull 1,141 times its own body weight. That would be like a person pulling 180,000 pounds (81,650 kg)!

FACT

The mantis shrimp is just 4 inches (10 centimeters) long. But it's incredibly strong. The shrimp can **accelerate** its club-like body parts fast enough to break the glass in most aquariums.

accelerate—to increase the speed of a moving object

CHAPTER 3

STRENGTH ENHANCEMENTS

People don't have Superman's strength. But scientists and engineers are working on increasing human strength. The Human Universal Load Carrier (HULC) helps soldiers carry heavy loads in combat. This **exoskeleton** allows users to carry up to 200 pounds (91 kg) with little effort.

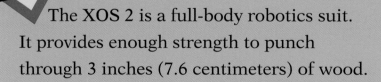

FACT

The XOS 2 is a full-body robotics suit. It provides enough strength to punch through 3 inches (7.6 centimeters) of wood.

Exoskeleton devices can help soldiers and factory workers lift and carry heavy loads.

exoskeleton—a metal device worn on a person's body that provides extra strength and support to do work

Exoskeletons can also help **paralyzed** people. Scientists have created specialized devices for people with spinal cord injuries. These devices provide hip and knee motion to help people stand and walk.

Exoskeleton devices can help patients learn to walk again.

paralyzed—unable to move or feel a part of the body

The Man of Steel is stronger than any human. People can't match Superman's muscles. But the science of strength is helping them test their limits. People may one day achieve feats of strength we can't imagine today.

GLOSSARY

accelerate (ak-SEL-uh-rayt)—to increase the speed of a moving object

exoskeleton (ek-soh-SKE-luh-tuhn)—a metal device worn on a person's body that provides extra strength and support to do work

gravity (GRAV-uh-tee)—a force that pulls objects together

involuntary (in-VOL-uhn-tehr-ee)—done without a person's control

nerve (NURV)—a thin fiber that carries messages between the brain and other parts of the body

paralyzed (PA-ruh-lized)—unable to move or feel a part of the body

resistance (ri-ZISS-tuhnss)—a force that opposes or slows the motion of an object

technology (tek-NOL-uh-jee)—the use of science to do practical things

tendon (TEN-duhn)—a strong, thick cord of tissue that joins a muscle to a bone

voluntary (VOL-uhn-ter-ee)—to choose to do something on purpose

READ MORE

Brett, Flora. *Your Muscular System Works!* Your Body Systems. North Mankato, Minn.: Capstone Press, 2015.

Labrecque, Ellen. *Strength: Build Muscles and Climb High!* Exercise! Chicago: Heinemann Library, 2013.

INTERNET SITES

FactHound offers a safe, fun way to find Internet sites related to this book. All of the sites on FactHound have been researched by our staff.

Here's all you do:
Visit *www.facthound.com*
Type in this code: 9781515750994

INDEX

bones, 8, 10

elephants, 15
exercise, 12
exoskeletons, 18, 20

gorillas, 15

horned dung beetles, 16

mantis shrimp, 17
muscles, 4, 6, 10, 12, 13, 21
  biceps, 10
  eye muscles, 7
  involuntary muscles, 7
  skeletal muscles, 7, 8, 9
  triceps, 10
  voluntary muscles, 7

nerves, 10

strength training, 12

tendons, 8

READ THEM ALL!

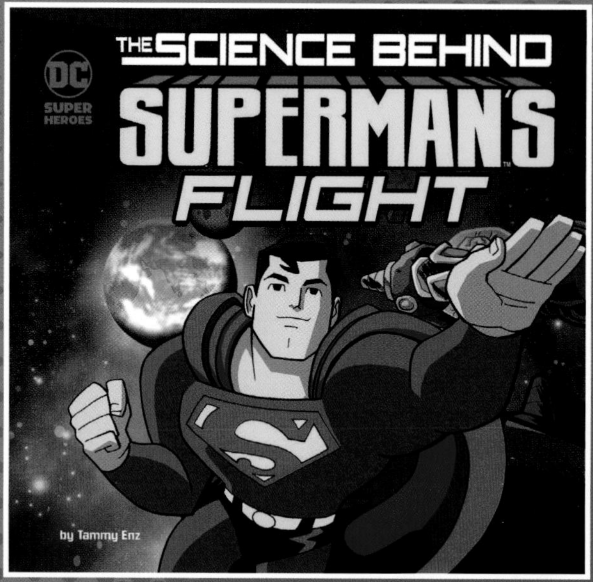
DC SUPER HEROES
THE SCIENCE BEHIND
SUPERMAN'S™
FLIGHT
by Tammy Enz

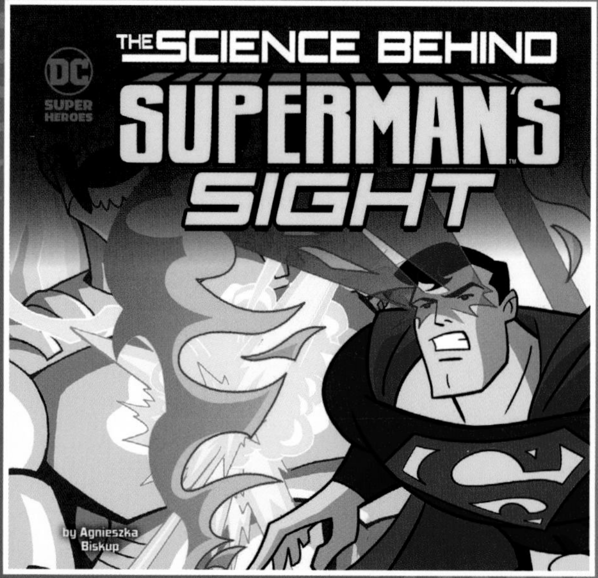
DC SUPER HEROES
THE SCIENCE BEHIND
SUPERMAN'S™
SIGHT
by Agnieszka Biskup

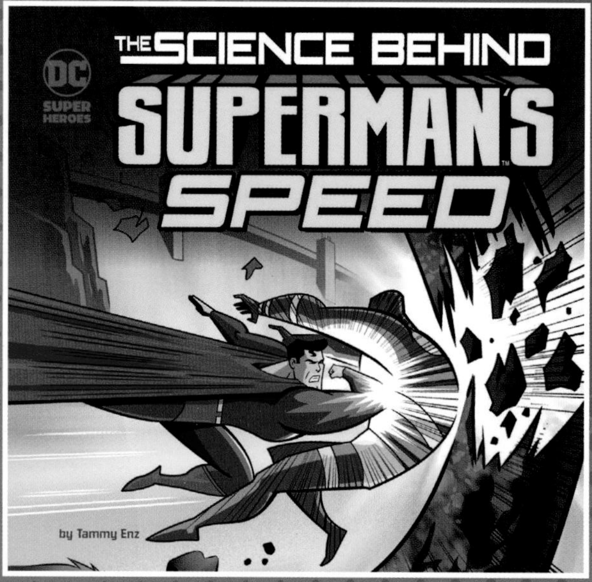
DC SUPER HEROES
THE SCIENCE BEHIND
SUPERMAN'S™
SPEED
by Tammy Enz

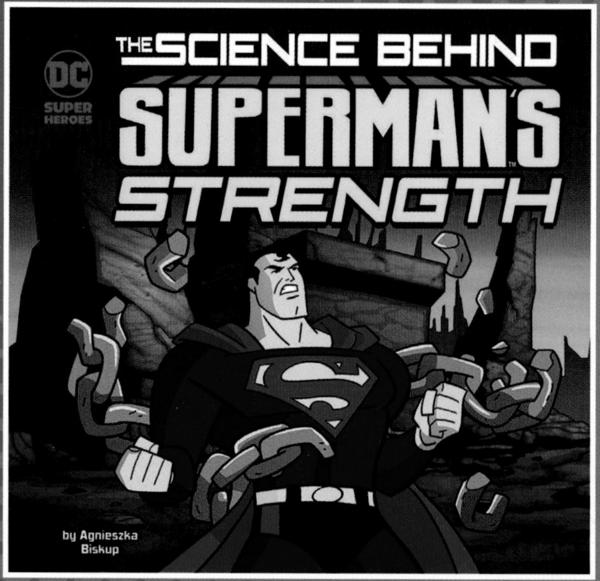
DC SUPER HEROES
THE SCIENCE BEHIND
SUPERMAN'S™
STRENGTH
by Agnieszka Biskup